BURY YOUR DEAD

The Long, Strange History of Death and Burial

by
S. Lewis

<u>*Bury Your Dead...*</u>
<u>*The Long, Strange History of*</u>
<u>*Death and Burial*</u>
Copyright ©2021 by S. Lewis
All rights reserved.
No part of this publication may be reproduced, stored in a retrieval system or transmitted in any way by any means, electronic, mechanical, photocopy, recording or otherwise without the prior permission of the author except as provided by USA copyright law.
Proper Publishing
P.O. Box 634
Cantonment, FL 32533
www.properpublishing.info
theproperpublisher@yahoo.com
Interior photos:
Adobe Photos
Needpix
Pixabay
WikiCommon

--*Information in this book was gathered from many different sources and as much as the author tried to ensure factual accuracy, the information should be used for entertainment purposes only.*

Contents

"No one here gets out alive."
— Jim Morrison

Approximately 10 years ago I found
myself standing in a funeral home,
paying my respects to a friend whose
family member had died. As I looked
around, it suddenly hit me how truly
strange the entire "production" of
burial is and the bizarre rituals we
participate in without questioning their
origin.
As soon as I got home, I began slowly
compiling information on the history of
mourning rituals and burial.
It has been a truly fascinating endeavor
that has changed how I view the most
mundane aspects of life.
I hope you enjoy sharing the weird
little bits of knowledge you'll gain from
this book.

Moment of Death

When it comes to the moment of death and the hours immediately following, many of our modern-day practices are rooted in fear and superstition.

Closing the decedents eyes is a good example.

The earliest burial rituals and customs were an attempt to satisfy the spirits who were thought to have been the cause of death. The eyes, considered "windows" to the spirit world, were shut to protect the living.

But from what? Did those who held this belief think the moment a person died, the spirit leaving created a vacuum within the body?

In Britain, the level-headed individual believed the eyes of the recent deceased were closed because eyelids were one of the first parts of the body affected by rigor mortis. Unless they were shut immediately after death, they would be stuck open due to rigor.

However, those who were superstitious believed that having a corpse look at you would be a threat to you or your family's mortality. Which is also why pennies were occasionally placed on eyelids…to hold them shut.

Maybe there was a hope that closing the eyes kept living souls from being pulled inside the now-empty vessel. Or fear that a multitude of spirits could exit from eyes not closed quickly enough and begin haunting the now bereaved family.

Covering the face with a cloth came from a similar fear.

Covered corpses

The pagan religion held the belief that at the moment of death, the soul escaped from the mouth. Which begs the question; was the intent to hold the soul inside or keep the soul from returning once it had left? And what happened once the cover was removed? Was that fear reserved for immediately following death only?

In many cultures, the same word is used for 'spirit' and 'breath' which indicates the depth of respect and understanding with the connection between breath and life.

The Greeks use 'pneuma' for *breath* or *blast of air* which is also loosely translated to *spirit*. 'Spiritus' is Latin for both *breath* and *spirit*. In Hebrew, 'ruach' means *wind, breath* or *spirit*. The Arabic word 'rouh' is *breathing deeply* and *spirit*. But the most interesting has to be the Sanskrit word, 'prana'…which translates to *breath, life force* and *vital energy*.

Another interesting superstition based solely on breath has to do with passing by cemeteries. This unusual belief is that you must hold your breath

whenever you're near a graveyard,
otherwise a restless spirit will enter
you. That sounds doable unless you
plan to go anywhere near Najaf, Iraq.
Najaf happens to be home to the largest
cemetery in the world. At 1,485 acres,
holding over five million bodies…you
would have to hold your breath for a
long, long, long time.

1,485-acre cemetery in Najar, Iraq

And is there a timeline for when
the soul finally leaves the body?
According to the Hindu religion, when
the soul passes out of the body, it
lingers near its original form and
familiar places for 10 days, called
'Preta' during this time. On the 11th
day, it begins its journey to Yama Loka,

to be judged by Lord Yama, the God of Death, which takes one full year.

And the Apayao believed it took 40 days for the spirit of the deceased to find its way. A belief which originated from the Roman Catholic religion, mirroring the ascension and resurrection of Jesus Christ.

Closing all doors and opening every window at the location of the death of a loved one is an old-world custom.

Why shut doors and open windows at the moment of death? The belief was that upon the soul's departure, should doors remain open, the person's spirit would become lost and wander the home looking for the way out forever. If all of the doors were closed and only windows stood open, the soul would be shuttled out of the dwelling and find its way to the next realm. A peaceful transition for everyone involved. But at its core, fear of being visited by a tortured spirit was the motive for this act.

An interesting add-on to this tradition is that some of its deepest roots can be found in Denmark, Sweden, Norway and the other Northern Countries in that region. A subtle combination of Christian and Pagan beliefs blend nature with tradition and faith. Which becomes a symbolic gesture of letting go while allowing life's vitality to comfort, permeating the gloom. Lit candles in windows are a common sight, lending to the ever-present belief that a light in the dark will lead a soul home.

Covering all of the mirrors with dark cloth is a practice that has been handed down generation after generation.

Covering mirrors at the moment of death

There are a few reasons this might be done. The most reasonable of them is to keep the mourners from seeing their own reflection, which allowed them to grieve without care, their appearance of no concern.

Another reason could be the long-held belief that a mirror doesn't cast a reflection but instead is a window to your soul. So, should a non-corporeal soul pass a mirror, the assumption is they would be so distressed at the realization of their own death they would wander the house, traumatized forever.

A 16th Century belief was at the moment of death, when the soul exited the shell of the body, a mirror could trap and hold them until the devil happened along to take them away.

And the most morbid and perhaps strangest reason is linked to Irish superstition which says the first person to catch their reflection in a mirror at the home of the deceased, will be the next to die. Interestingly enough, Victorians believed something similar. They held fast to the idea that anyone catching sight of their reflection in a mirror in the same room where someone had passed would die soon, also.

Stopping the clocks and covering all clock faces is another interesting tradition that originated in Germany and Great Britain. What could the belief propelling this behavior be? Stopping a clock at the moment of death signifies time has now stopped for the deceased and their loved ones. When the person that died was the head of the household, the clocks would be stopped and would never be started again. The lyrics of the Johnny Cash song, "My Grandfather's Clock" tells of this tradition in such a beautifully mournful way:

My grandfather's clock was too large
for the shelf
so, it stood ninety years on the floor.
It was taller by half than the old man himself
though it weighed not a pennyweight more.
It was bought on the morn
of the day he was born
and was always his treasure and pride.
But it stopped, short, never to go again
when the old man died.

In Europe and America, in the 1800's, family photographs containing the image of the now deceased loved one were sometimes turned face-down to protect the friends and relatives from possession by the spirit of the dead.

The overwhelming fear of returning spirits could, at times, be taken to extremes.

In early England, the Saxons cut off the feet of the deceased, forever taking away their ability to walk. Many aborigine tribes took it one step further (pun intended) and decapitated the recently departed. The rational being the spirit would then be too busy looking for its head to bother the living. Makes you wonder if the Irish writer, Bram Stoker had somehow heard about this little ritual when he wrote his novel "Dracula".

Some cultures burned the home of the deceased to keep their spirit from returning to that place.

In the 1800's, it was common for a family to insist a deceased relative be carried from the house feet first.

There were two possible reasons for this; both of which were equally macabre.

One reason was to prevent the spirit from seeing the house and convincing another family member to follow them.

The second reason could be because the spirit couldn't see where he was going and so would be unable to retrace his steps. Although, if this were a Saxon household, how could they retrace their steps without the benefit of actual feet?

However, modern day coroners still follow the 'feet-first' practice of body removal for one simple rule: a body in rigor is easier to bend at the knees than trying to force the large muscles of the upper body to move around corners.

There are some rituals which seem to have crossed oceans.

The ancient Greeks believed at the moment of death the spirit of the person left the body as a single breath. Similarly, in ancient Rome, when a death occurred at home, the closest relative would make every attempt to inhale the final breath.

So, was the intent to capture the escaping spirit and somehow keep it close? Or maybe there was some desire for a temporary possession, perhaps hoping for a final word or thought from the newly deceased relative? The idea seems so odd but with the proper belief in place, anything can be seen as rational.

Ancient yogis incorporated breathing routines into exercise and relaxation thousands of years before the Roman Empire. They understood on a profound level that breath is life.

One more ritual both the Greeks and Roman's shared was placing a coin under the deceased person's tongue. The coin was payment for Charon, the ferryman of the river Styx, which was the boundary between the living world and the underworld. If Charon didn't have his ferry money, the soul wouldn't be ferried to the underworld, left to wander forever.

The practice can also be found in 17th Century Wales, North of England,

where the coins were placed with the
deceased "to give to St. Peter."

Saxon coin

By far, the moment of death
ritual that has an origin which could
claim the title "most macabre" comes
from ancient Egypt.

The act of praying or reading from
a sacred book at the bedside of the
dying or deceased. Praying for a loved
one's soul is a response from family
members to 'save' the individual from a
perceived 'eternal damnation.'

Egyptians, both common and
royal, engaged in reading sacred spells
from "The Book of the Dead", hoping
to guide souls to the Hall of Truth and
eventual judgement from the god
Osiris.

The Book of the Dead

Osiris weighed the heart of the deceased against the white feather of Ma'at, (truth and harmony.) If the heart was lighter than a feather, they were admitted into the Field of Reeds (Egyptian paradise) where they experienced an eternity of their life as it was on earth. If the heart was heavier than the feather, it was thrown to the god Amut where it was eaten, which erased the soul of the person, altogether. By far, the worst fate imaginable for the soul of an Egyptian was non-existence.

So, the next time someone begins reciting prayers and quoting scripture, remember, it all started with the "Book of the Dead" and the white feather of truth and harmony.

For the majority of recorded history, individual beliefs were based, in part at least, on the interpretations set forth by certain authority figures; namely shaman, priests, medicine men and spirit talkers. A personal understanding that ghosts are evil spirits or divine links to other worlds, would then influence their community to believe the same. Leaving entire societies convinced deceased persons brought about either catastrophic circumstances or enlightened moments, depending on what was set forth by the spiritual advisors in charge. Which is why the beliefs regarding death and spirituality can vary drastically from region to region. It isn't that they are based on a holy doctrine; instead, they are founded primarily on superstition and fear.

How do we know this? Because the location of the 'spirit body' seems to reflect so perfectly with the culture of those who have died.

The Native American Zuni's

spirit home was a flurry of happy activity in a "Dance Village". While the Tlingit Indians went to a "Ghosts' Home" following the entire village participating in a Potlatch ceremony. The islanders of New Caledonia believed their spirit world, known as Tsiabiloum, was located beneath the ocean.

Tlingit dancers at a Potlatch ceremony

Grief/Mourning Rituals

So much of what is now considered tradition is rooted in atonement, fear or status. All of which seem to hold sway over the history of many of our "normal" rituals to some degree.

The consumption of food and drink after a funeral has some interesting origins.

From the early 1600's to the early 1900's, families paid to have the deceased's sins taken away prior to burial. "Sin-eaters" and "sin-eating" was commonplace across the British Isles. In rural parts of England, Scotland and Wales, after the death of a loved one, a piece of bread would be placed on the face or chest of the deceased as an offering. The family would then send for the village sin-eater.

While loved ones crowded around the corpse, drinking and

mourning, the professional sin-eater would consume the offering, which symbolized taking on the sins of the deceased, allowing them unfettered entry into the afterlife.

All negative behavior having been passed on to the sin-eater, he would recite a prayer over the body;

"I give easement and rest now to thee, dear man/woman. Come not down the lanes or in our meadows. And for thy peace, I pawn my own soul. Amen."

Due to the religious climate, at that time, the idea of sin holding a person back from Heaven was unacceptable.

Sin-eaters were a necessity for rural villages but taking on that profession meant being shunned by the community and living in obscurity for fear of execution by the church.

Scholars trace the origin of sin-eating, historically, to pagan traditions. However, there was a medieval custom where nobility gave food to the poor as payment for prayers said on behalf of the deceased. In 1712, Henry Curzon wrote that villagers in an English county hired "poor people to take on them the Sins of the Deceased," for the Catholic holiday All Souls' Day, which, in essence, reduced an entire social class to sin-eating.

Another unique grief-driven ritual involving eating can be found with some cultures in Papua New Guinea and the Wari tribes in Brazil. They practiced 'endocannibalism', which was also called the 'feast of the dead'. It was a way for loved ones to permanently connect with their deceased family member. Those cultures felt they honored the dead by eating them; it was their way of coping with the fear and horror of death and grief. Those societal beliefs revolved around this final gesture of love from the tribe and family, as they believed endocannibalism was something the dead expected of the living.

Most people assume wearing black as a sign of mourning goes back to the Victorian era, however, that is untrue.

In ancient Rome, dark togas were worn by those in mourning, and the practice of wearing dark clothing (and sometimes white) was common in Europe during the Middle Ages and through the Renaissance period.

In the early 1800's, when a death occurred, the carpenter was immediately called to build a coffin. The deceased would be laid out, dressed in a shroud for viewing by friends and family, and the burial was done as soon as possible after a quick funeral service. However, when the Consort of the British Monarch, Prince Albert died in 1861 at the age of 42, Queen Victoria's extravagant 40-year-long mourning period brought about the era of Victorian mourning customs and 'proper grieving.'

The daughters of Prince Albert and Queen Elizabeth in deep mourning.

Fashion magazines outlined rules of 'proper etiquette and clothing' for mourning.

The attire seemed simple…for men. They wore a black suit, black armband and a wide black hat band the day of the funeral for his wife and three days following. After that, his life went back to normal and he was encouraged to remarry as soon as possible. For women, it wasn't that simple. Etiquette and societal rules required her to be in deep mourning for her husband for the first year and allowed half-mourning for the following year. What was 'deep mourning?' The woman had to wear an entire wardrobe of black crepe. Gloves, handkerchiefs and under-clothes were all dull black, devoid of embellishments such as lace or bows. She had to wear a veil whenever in public, as well as no jewelry for the first year. During half-mourning, black jewelry was permitted. No social activities and absolutely no laughter.

All members of the house were also in deep mourning. Children wore black, infants were dressed in white with black trim and ribbons. Curtains remained drawn, clocks were stilled, and mirrors covered. Black crepe or a black wreath hung from the front door. After a suitable amount of time, she would send out black-edged cards announcing the end of her grieving and visitors were welcome. Traditions to honor a deceased person could bring villages, towns, communities together in an effort to both appease the spirits and ease the pain of grief.

There still seems to be a belief that the number of mourners and depth of grief displayed is an accurate indicator to the importance of the deceased person. Where did this strange little belief come from?

Professional mourners have been found in many countries and is an ancient tradition which can also be found in the Old and New Testaments.

"Thus says the Lord of hosts, Consider and call for the mourning women, That they may come; And send for the wailing women, That they may come: Let them make haste and take up a wailing for us,

That our eyes may shed tears and our eyelids flow with water." (Jeremiah 9:17-18)
"Therefore thus says the Lord God of hosts, the Lord, There is wailing in all the plazas, and in all the streets they say, 'Alas! Alas!' They also call the farmer to mourning and professional mourners to lamentation." (Amos 5:16)

The unusual practice of paying mourners has been traced back to China and the Middle East, but there were also indications in Ancient Egypt and Rome.

The professional mourners of Mani, Greece

Women were the most acceptable to hire. Men were supposed to be strong leaders of families and therefore it was socially unacceptable for men express extreme emotions due to pride. Women, on the other hand, were ideal as it was socially acceptable for them to express such strong emotions as grief.

Professional mourners

The link between mourning and religious belief was also a catalyst for hiring mourners. Individuals who showed themselves to be especially "good" at wailing were paid to attend more funerals and were expected to perform with much moaning.

In late 15th Century, William Courtney, the Archbishop of Canterbury, paid to have 15,000 masses be said to speed his soul through purgatory after his death in 1496. The reigning monarch at the time, Henry VII, could only afford 10,000 masses said on his behalf.

Think about that the next time you roll your eyes at an overly enthusiastic display of grief at a funeral. Maybe they are just what was ordered for the occasion.

A specific place for photos or items belonging to the deceased individual, resembling a shrine of sorts goes all the way back to the beginning of religion.

Veneration of the dead or ancestor veneration, in one form or another, has been found in every culture although most did not classify it as "ancestor worship." It was regarded more as loving respect and a way to ask for help and protection for living descendants.

The Chinese character for filial piety is called "xiao."

It is the oldest character within their written language and was found painted on ox bones which were dated to approximately 1000 BCE. The original meaning being, *providing food offerings to one's ancestors.* The character is a depiction of its meaning, which is a combination of the characters *lao*, which means old, and *er zi*, which means son. *Lao* being the top-half of the character, *er zi* being the bottom-half. The character itself shows the older generation being carried by the younger generation, which goes directly to the heart of what the Chinese philosopher, Confucius believed was critical for a peaceful family and successful society.

The honoring of elders and long-dead ancestors is a tenet which hastened divine worship. So, maybe that family Bible really does belong with the framed photos of your dead relatives. One actually brought about the other.

Most Native American cultures looked at death not as an ending, but more as a continuation of a journey. During actual mourning, loved ones would express their loss in extreme fashion, wailing, crying, screaming, singing, cutting off their hair and slashing at their own bodies. The funerary ritual for Lakota people lasted two days and was a long, exhausting event culminating in a community coming together to honor and show great respect for the loved one now moving on.

A lock of the deceased persons hair would be held over burning sweetgrass for purification, then wrapped in sacred buckskin while a Sacred Pipe was smoked. The bundle of sacred buckskin wrapped hair, called a "soul bundle" was kept safe in the tipi of the soul's keeper…most often a relative of the deceased. That special individual, called the Keeper of the Soul, vowed a harmonious life until the release of the soul, which usually occurred after a year.

The sacred bundle would be carried outside and the moment it reached open air the soul was then deemed released. If it was judged worthy, it was sent to the right, to Wakan Tanka. If unworthy, it would be sent to the left where it remained until eventually gaining purification and joining Wakan Tanka.

An interesting aspect of Lakota grief is that it was considered something to be valued. Sorrow was thought to bring people closer to God, because when someone suffered loss and was in the midst of great grief, they were also considered "most holy." During that time, their prayers were thought to have power and others in the village would ask those grieving to pray on their behalf.

36

Burial

The act of burying a loved one has been traced back to Mesopotamia, in ancient Sumer in 5000 BCE. Although the oldest known burial has been linked to "The Red Lady" who was dated at 24,000 BC.

Sumarians believed that the afterlife was a dark foreboding place, and it was helpful to provide the deceased with easy transition to that gloomy underworld by placing them physically closer. It was deeply held that those who did not have a respectable burial, returned to haunt living relatives, similar to modern day stories of spirits causing problems in homes or possessing objects or people. Again, fear being the driving force behind ensuring a loved one is buried appropriately.

One of the most common phrases we use today came directly from 4500 BCE. burial practices. Individual graves containing tools and personal possessions were discovered in the Neolithic village of Banpo. Although it is not known if any rituals were performed, the existence of items considered important to the individual during life, also showed a belief of continued existence in an afterlife. Proper burial, and divine harmony was of the utmost importance when aiming to help their loved ones peacefully rest hoping to prevent a haunting by an angry ghost. Hence…rest in peace. R.I.P. Which was literally a plea to their loved ones to lie down and sleep contentedly instead of rising in restlessness to wander forever tortured. Maybe that fear was a 500-year carry-over from the Sumarians.

Often referred to as 'grave goods', items have been placed with deceased loved ones and powerful individuals for thousands of years. Pottery, tools, flowers and carvings

have been located in ancient burial sites
all over the world.

The practice of putting flowers in
or on a place of burial seems to have
come from the practical idea that the
smell of the flowers would cover the
odor of the body decaying. However,
there was also a superstition regarding
flowers and graves; if a grave had
wildflowers grow naturally, it was
believed the deceased had moved on to
heaven because they had a 'good soul'.
Adversely, if the grave was dusty and
barren, it was a signal of a dark soul
that had been dragged to hell. Both
beliefs evolved to artificial flowers now
decorating modern graves.

Other instances of interesting
'grave goods' are the thousands of life-
size clay soldiers with horses and
wooden chariots which were found in
an elaborate mausoleum constructed
during the Han dynasty, while Qin Shi
Huang Di was the First Emperor of
Qin.

The clay army of the Qin mausoleum

The mausoleum was constructed while he was alive, and building was halted due to an uprising after his death in 209 BC.

Think about those life-size soldiers the next time you see someone with a pile of stuff in the coffin with them. Could be worse…could be an entire army.

Headstones and grave markers are a common sight around the globe but the reasons for them are as varied as the styles you see walking through your local cemetery. Tombstones, initially, were used because it was believed that spirits, namely ghosts, could be weighed down, held in place so they could not rise up and haunt those still living.

Which is why the layout of older cemeteries are maze-like. They believed ghosts could only travel in straight lines, so the paths in cemeteries were winding and made to, hopefully, keep the spirits confined to their burial place. The ringing of bells, firing of guns and wailing were all used in their time to scare ghosts away from retreating loved ones, as the fear of following spirits was ever present.

Mourning bells

Although the pyramids and elaborate tombs of China, Egypt and Mayan cultures don't necessarily come to mind when you think of 'headstone', they are, in fact, burial markers. The notion of having a bigger grave marker meaning you're more important truly goes back thousands of years. Kings, Queens, Pharaoh's, all needed to show their grandeur, plus there was a strong belief in securing your place in the afterlife. The Moai statues at Easter Island are also markers. Those 86-ton megaliths each represent chieftains or other important people who passed away. The bigger the statue, the more it cost the village, which obviously equates to more love and greater respect. So, in the end, it always goes back to that old adage: "Bigger is better."

The Moai statues of Easter Island

Stonehenge has long been considered a Neolithic calendar marking Summer Solstice. However, for well over a thousand years the builders and their ancestors buried their dead in huge earthen barrows, with the long mounds pointing toward the lunar northern and southern risings. Common in Neolithic Britain, bones of children and adults were located in ditches at the ends of both entrances.

Extreme displays of love and loyalty included Sati or Suttee, which is the Ritual of Widow Burning, and is exactly that…upon the husband's death, the widow sits atop the funerary pyre and immolates herself as her husband is cremated.

*Sati handprints, Mehrangarh,
Jodhpur, Rajasthan, India*

It was believed that spiritually they would never part, which lead to the name Sati, which loosely translates to *faithful wife* or *good wife*.

Making memorial cards, having quilts made from the deceased's clothes, clipping some hair or nails; all go to the heart of wanting to keep the person alive, or have a part of them close.

This desire is found as far back as burial itself, however the ways in which people have chosen to act on this urge has changed drastically over the years.

In the Middle Ages (5th-15th century) death masks gained popularity for memorializing the dead. Clay, plaster and wax were all materials used at the time, and while gruesome, sculptors and painters used them for reference. At the time, law enforcement used death masks to document the faces of unidentified bodies. In the 1800's and 1900's death masks of the famous and infamous became all the rage.

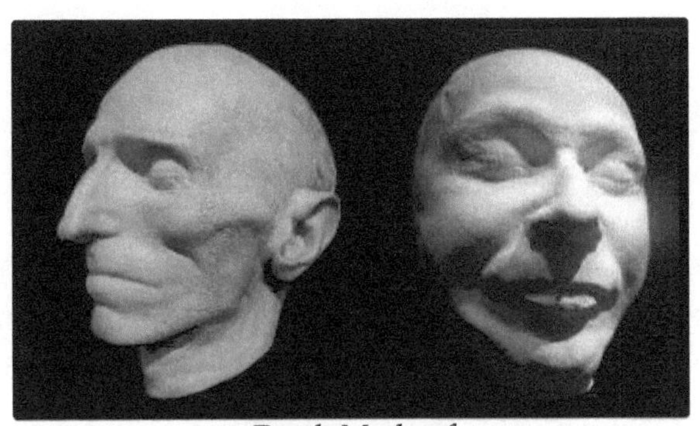

Death Masks of
Nikola Tesla and Heinrich Himmler

At that time also, Victorian post-mortem photography came into fashion.

In some instances, just the deceased individual was in the photo, however it was much more common to see an entire family, posing with their now-dead loved one. Special forms and racks were constructed to fit under clothes, behind curtains or bedding to hold the deceased loved one in whatever pose the family wished. Giving them the opportunity to have one last photograph, or in some instances the only photograph, of their loved one, before burial. Sometimes, the staging was done so well, it was impossible to determine which person in the photo was deceased. Which brings us to current times when we gaze at deceased loved ones during viewings and comment on how it only looks like they are sleeping. Our unwillingness to accept what is right in front of us has pushed our society to "mask death" with make-up, wigs, nice clothes and jewelry all in an attempt to deny the finality of the moment.

The one piece of information that seems impossible is that a belief which was classified as a societal obligation somehow managed to travel 7,000 miles.

The Ancient Greeks carved stones in remembrance of individuals, to honor what they had done over the course of their life. Remembrance of the dead was crucial and was dictated according to Eusebia, or 'piety'. Eusebia was a kind of doctrine on how young people treated their elders, how slaves interacted with masters, how wives were treated by their husbands…basically it was a guide for how someone acted toward their superiors. This also carried over into respecting those who had died, as well as the souls of those individuals.

Exactly like the Ancient Chinese practice of filial piety. Which was the belief that the younger generation had an obligation to take care of and honor those that came before them, whether alive or not.

How did two entirely separate ancient societies located 7,000 miles apart, believe the exact same thing at the exact same moment in time?

Burial is only one option for a deceased loved one transitioning from one world to the next.

Cremation has been an active part of death and mourning around the world for thousands of years. The Balinese see cremation as an occasion for celebration, since it is a holy duty finally fulfilled. In 2008, the Island of Bali had one of its most lavish cremation ceremonies ever as Agung Suyasa, head of the royal family, was cremated, along with almost 70 commoners. Thousands of celebrating volunteers carried a massive bamboo platform containing Suyasa's body, they also carried a large wooden bull and a wooden dragon. After a long, winding procession, Suyasa's body was placed inside the wooden bull and burned while the wooden dragon watched his soul find release by fire.

In the Northwestern Philippines, the Benguet people place blindfolds over the eyes of their deceased and sit them next to the main entrance to their homes. While the Caviteno, near Manila, place their dead in hollowed-out tree trunks. The Tinguian people dress their deceased loved ones in the finest clothes, sit them in a chair and light a cigarette for them to enjoy. The Apayao…well they just put their loved ones under the kitchen.

So, how did burial take place during plagues? Mass graves were organized in larger cities where the death tolls were enormous. "Plague Pits" were so common they have long been forgotten. The Meadows, in Edinburgh, was the location of one of those mass graves, and is now used as a public park. Charterhouse in Smithfield was London's biggest plague pit, thought to contain 50,000 victims.

Ancient mounds dot the landscape of the eastern half of the United States. One of the most notable being the Serpent mound in Adams County, Ohio which is 1,348 feet long and 2,500 years old. Called effigy mounds, they date as far back as 500 B.C. to as recently as 1500 A.D. and were created by innumerable American Indian societies.

The first mounds were discovered in the late 1700's, early 1800's by settlers and explorers who were spreading out across America. The beliefs about the origins of these mounds varied wildly from being constructed by Vikings, to the 10 Lost Tribes of Israel, to Atlanteans.

We know why most societies bury, cremate, or mummify the way they do...all except for one. The Bo people of the Hemp Pond Valley in Southwest China's Gongxian County were a vivacious society. Strong and active, they thrived until they were massacred by the Ming Dynasty over

five centuries ago. The only thing left of
their time on this planet are the 160
black coffins which extend out from a
rock face 300 feet above the ground.
Placed along high cliffs and within
natural caves, some of the wooden
casket's rest on posts that jut out from
the cliff itself. Today, locals refer to the
'Bo People' as *Sons of the Cliffs* and
Subjugators of the Sky but their reason
for displaying their dead in such a way
will forever remain a mystery.

Southwest China, the Bo people
suspended coffins on a cliffside.

One of our own presidents,
Thomas Jefferson was so intrigued, he
excavated one of the mounds located

near his home in central Virginia. Estimating it contained more than 1,000 American Indian skeletons, his curiosity led him to unearth a giant burial mound.

After Death

The funeral or celebration of life ceremonies seem to have taken on a life of their own and in some instances last many years. Whether choosing to say goodbye in a quiet, somber fashion or dancing through the streets to a jazz band, the reasons are the same…a deep respect for the deceased.

Veneration of the dead is a reoccurring theme. The ways in which different cultures choose to honor their ancestors are as varied as the people themselves.

In Madagascar, five years after a loved one dies, the entire family visits the ancestral burial place to exhume all of those interred. Families dance and request blessings. The loved ones are then re-wrapped and put back in the family crypt until the next "Famadihana" or *Turning of the Bones*.

Celebrating with deceased loved ones

Similarly, in Indonesia, a Torajan family will save for years so they can afford an extravagant funeral. Expenses can be so grand that the funeral could take place years after the actual death. The family simply states their loved one *"is sleeping"* or *"feeling sick"* and the family carries on as if nothing has changed. Dressing and taking their *"sick"* loved one with them on outings, the family and village continues on until the funeral is paid for and only then does the "sick" individual finally die, becoming the focus of great sorrow and grief.

In South Korea, a law was passed in 2000 requiring families to remove the remains of loved ones from burial crypts after 60 years due to a shortage of burial space. That has drastically increased the number of cremations; however, ashes aren't always the first option.

Many companies have started compressing the remains into gem-like stones which can then be displayed as Death Beads
on a small shrine to the deceased, hung somewhere special in the home…or perhaps worn.

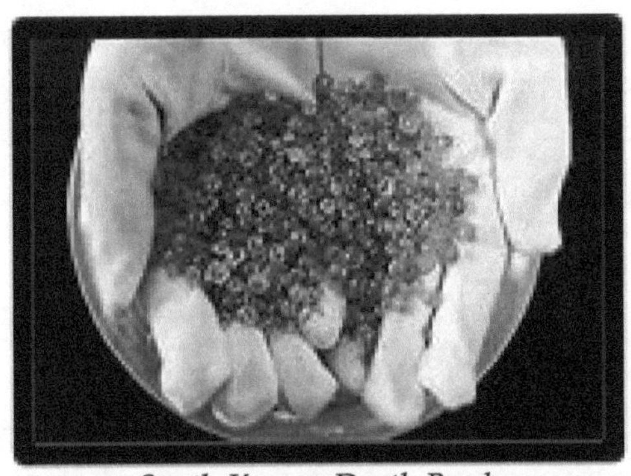
South Korean Death Beads

The jazz funerals of New Orleans fuse African American, French and West African traditions. Sorrowful tunes play until after the burial, when the music becomes upbeat and celebratory. Dancing to honor their now deceased loved one, family members are often joined by their community, as the music helps them share in the joy of life and pain of death.

In North America, the Native American nations believed that their rituals helped the soul leave the body and it took four days for the departed to ascend to their own nirvana. However, ritual traditions depended largely on region.

It was not uncommon for it to take up to a year to bury a loved one in the Sioux tribe, although they would be dressed in the best clothes, and stored in a hollow tree in the meantime.

When the Iroquois lost a warrior in battle, they would engage in "mourning wars." Which were raids on their enemy to take back one of their tribesmen who had been held captive. Basically, it was Red Rover in real-life.

Incas felt that a person never really died unless they were forgotten, which is why most mummified remains became family advisers or trusted confidantes. It makes perfect sense…it's not as if they were going to share anything they were told.

The Mayans would dig vertical shafts into the ground, burying the dead under their own huts, along with a few livestock, and slaves. Only the important people had tombs build for them.

Taphephobia is the clinical term for the fear of being buried while still alive.

Chopin, George Washington, Hans Christian Anderson, and Alfred Nobel are just four examples of individuals plagued with such a fear. At that time in the 19th century, determining death was based more on guesswork than actual science.

Chopin was so fearful he insisted with his last known words: "Swear to make them cut me open, so I won't be buried alive." He made it clear to his family that upon declaration of his death, his heart must be removed, and that organ alone be buried in his homeland, Poland.

George Washington insisted his seemingly deceased body be laid out for three days, to ensure he was in fact dead.

Hans Christian Anderson and Alfred Nobel both instructed that after they were presumed dead, their veins were to be opened and their bodies drained, to ensure their death.

Unfortunately, there have been documented cases of people actually buried alive.

In the mid-1880's, a young lady named Anna was dressing for her brother's wedding, and while waiting, sat down to rest. When a family member checked on her several minutes later, she was still there – "head leaning against the wall and apparently lifeless".

When aid arrived, the doctor assumed she was dead. Anna's nervous nature and the fact that she suffered from heart palpitations was the determined cause of death. However, this didn't sit well with some of her friends, who commented to each other on how her ears still looked as though blood was flowing through them. Buried the next day, her friends told her parents of their observation. Of course, this alarmed her parents and they had her dug back up. They indeed found the worst-case scenario: Anna's body was now turned on its side, fingers gnawed to the bone, and hair torn out by handfuls.

And then this article, taken from a newspaper dated March 15th, 1881:

A young lady died of small-pox, and according to the sanitary laws of Rumania she was buried at once. As she had been recently betrothed the presents of her lover were buried with her, according to the Rumanian custom. These presents consisted of jewels, and they excited the cupidity of three robbers, who went to the grave at night and dug up the coffin. When it was opened one of the robbers was afraid to touch the corpse, whereat his fellows jeered at him. At this he gave the head of the corpse a sound cuffing and let it drop. At the next instant the dead woman arose and said, "Don't kill me, I beg you." Naturally the robbers fled and the unfortunate girl arose and crawling from her grave, went home and was received with mingled terror and joy.

Afterlife

Without any scientific proof of existence, heaven and hell have reigned supreme when both common men and intellectuals discuss the likelihood of afterlife.

The notion of eternal reward or threat of everlasting punishment became commonplace, and that fear was a valuable resource for individuals hoping to guide the decisions and actions of others.

George Gallup founded the American Institute of Public Polling in the mid-30's. In 1944, the poll began asking American's their views on religion, the afterlife and opinions on what might await us once we die. For the last 60 years, the number of people that believe in heaven has remained steady at between 70% to 85%. Ironically, only 55% to 75% of Americans believe in hell. Now, our ideas of both of those 'places' change dramatically based on geographical location and religion. But one fact holds true across the board and that is the unknown about death can be terrifying. Any 'known' bits of information we have serve only to quell those fears. Not necessarily because they are based on fact but more so because they are based on hopeful assumption. Hopeful being the key word, there.

In Japan, Buddhist and Shintoist beliefs have hinged on purification through water and salt since the Bronze-Iron age (1200 BC-550 BC) and that same practice continues to this day. *Matsugo no Mizu* or 'water of the last moment' is used to wet the lips of the deceased. Tokens are then placed beside the body in the casket, which will allow them passage on the River Sanzu, where the dead are judged.

Most African religions recognized that life continued on but in a separate form. The dead give strength to the living which, in turn, strengthens their corporeal spirit. Unlike most religions, though, what is most important is what is occurring in the here and now.

The Aztec's had a complex set of beliefs about the afterlife. What was unique about their belief structure was it was based on how the person died rather than on the life they lead up to that point.

Women who died giving birth, people who died from disease, killed by lightning or drowning…they either helped the sun rise every morning or they went to a gloriously gorgeous place where they just ate and drank all day.

But if you died of natural causes like old age or you were killed in battle? You were going to spend years making your way through multiple levels of challenges to either finally be granted peace, or you got to return to Earth as a hummingbird. Wonder how many people stood outside during electrical storms hoping for that awesome afterlife?

Native American's were sprawled over so much territory, tribes had their own belief structures.

Tribes from the Plains called their afterlife *Happy Hunting Ground,* where there was always plenty of buffalo to hunt.

Pueblo Indians' believed everything was just a continuation; you went to a different area and met people who had died before. But there were no punishments, because this was just a journey continued. Lessons still to learn.

The Cheyenne believed their spirit had to find the trail where all of the footprints pointed in the same direction. Following the trail, they would go to the camp of the dead which was in the stars. There they would be reunited with friends and relatives who had already died.

A common theme among all of the Indian beliefs is reconnecting with those who went before.

But absolutely no afterlife is as awesome as the afterlife of the Viking warrior. *Valhalla,* which means 'The Hall of the Fallen' is a palace guarded by wolves and eagles. Welcomed by the god Odin, warriors ate wild boar and drank as much mead as they wanted. Battling each other for sport, warriors continue training for Ragnarok, or doomsday. If you weren't a warrior but died at sea or drowned, afterlife was at the hall of the god Aegir, who hosted parties for all of the other gods. For warriors who weren't lucky enough to make it to *Valhalla*, they found themselves in a meadow ruled by the goddess Freyja. They spent eternity telling stories, making art and being faithful companions to women who died as maidens. That sounds absolutely awful, doesn't it?

Valhalla

Ghost paths or death roads are perfectly straight and converge on a cemetery. Medieval tracks used for transporting corpses to burial, although long forgotten, were originally thought to be unique to the Netherlands. However, throughout many parts of northern Europe, researchers are finding traces of these death roads in folklore, and ancient archeological sites in Germany, Scandinavia, and Britain. Scholars now feel the origins lie in the Viking practice of carrying a dead chieftain to burial along a special, straight, ritual road.

Geisterwege which translates to "ghost paths" were found in parts of Germany. Always in the same place, anyone walking on them would often meet ghosts. Without exception, the paths run a straight line through mountains, valleys and marshes. Passing through towns, close by houses and in some cases, going right through them. Ending or originating at a cemetery, it is in fact considered "the place where the spirits of the deceased thrive" and definitely a place spoken of with hushed tones.

Current afterlife beliefs in America come from a blend of cultures and religions. Native American spirituality, soulful African heritage, the beauty of veneration from Spain, the deep emotional connection from the European heritage, all of our traditions have roots in so many small immigrant communities.

Hanging our history on one hook is impossible and does a disservice to all of the beauty that has been given to our heritage by other cultures.

Ancient Andean Mummy Bundle

Odds and Endings

I

Birds have been associated with death and the afterlife for thousands of years because of their ability to fly, leading man to believe that they were messengers to the gods. A number of superstitions surrounding birds have evolved over time, specifically regarding owls, vultures, ravens, and crows.

Whether you hear an owl hoot your name, vultures circle your home, a raven or crow enters your house, perches on your sill, or strikes a window…all signal a death which will soon visit your family. And all are dark omens. At least according to superstition.

II

There was a time, if a fire spat out a coffin shaped ember, that was a foretelling of death, as did doing laundry on New Years Day. That was a sure cause of death. As you were said to be 'washing one of the family away.'

III

It is also considered bad luck to transport a body in your own vehicle…do we really have to go into all of the questions around this superstition? And wouldn't it be worse luck to actually be the body in someone's vehicle?! It is also considered a dark omen to see your reflection in the windows of a hearse.

IV

In the 17th century, there was a long-held belief that the last image a person saw was somehow seared into the deceased person's eyes. However, it wasn't until 1878 that a man named Kuhne provided dramatic examples of 'imprinted images' on rabbits retinae after death. Further experiments in 1975 only served to muddle the line between science and superstition, which ultimately killed any further experiments. Pun intended.

V

And the final bit of interesting info…the term 'wake' has long been associated with the tradition of friends and family holding vigil over the deceased in the days before the funeral. Although most believe the term 'wake' refers to loved ones watching to ensure the deceased is in fact deceased…it does not.

It refers, instead, to the loved ones staying awake and keeping watch over the body as a show of devotion and love.

Headstone from 1878

Prologue

Veneration of the dead is still very much alive (yes, pun intended) just look at Dias de los Muertos. Mexico's Day of the Dead celebration is veneration of the dead at its best.

The reverence, celebratory nature and honor paid to those already dead is prevalent throughout the day. Families make beautiful alters in their homes, honoring their deceased loved ones. Flowers, candles, favorite foods and sweet breads decorate the alters. Celebrations continue in the cemetery, with picnics, music, dancing and families that spend the night with those they've lost. How old is the tradition? It can be traced back 3,000 years to the Aztec culture. Even surviving the arrival of the Spanish who thought the cultural ceremonies were sacrilegious. However, instead of doing away with the celebrations, it evolved to incorporate subtle Christian elements. Like changing the date to November

2nd, which is the Christian holiday of All Souls Day, also called the Feast of All Souls.

What is the take-away?

That for all of our strange traditions, they came from a place of good intentions.

From covering the face, to burial, to digging up long-dead relatives, it always goes back to the desire to honor those who have died. And that still holds true.

But keep in mind, labeling something 'tradition' doesn't lend to its validity. So much of what we do when it comes to death is based solely on fear.

Traditions can change over time and it's possible to embrace loss and grief without acknowledging the fears of our ancestors.

Or, at the very least, share what you've learned from this little book with others. Hopefully, it will help take away the pain and strangeness of our mourning rituals. And maybe replace it with a bit of wonder for the traditions and love that have carried our grief through the ages.

If you would like to order any books by S. Lewis, they are all available on Amazon or you may request a personalized copy from the author at the following email address, subject heading 'BOOK ORDER REQUEST':

theproperpublisher@yahoo.com

Titles by the author:

Goodbye, Mama
Racing the Past
The Issued Wife
Misfits, Hellraisers and Orphans
Hesitation Marks
The Happiness Habit
What Lies Between
A Little Florida Farm
Bury your Dead

About the author:

S. Lewis spends the majority of life in a creaky, old farmhouse. Renting rooms to spiders, ghosts and such, writing isn't a solitary experience in that drafty wooden structure.

Vacationing in mausoleums and admittedly addicted to the smell of mold, loamy earth, and decay...cemeteries offer all the hospitality needed for S. Lewis.

Mother to three daemons, wife to one ancient, evil creature and caretaker to many wild animals...she buries her dead daily.